YELLOW CLOVER

Katharine Coman

YELLOW CLOVER

A Book of Remembrance

BY

KATHARINE LEE BATES

AUTHOR OF "FAIRY GOLD,"
"THE RETINUE," ETC.

NEW YORK
E. P. DUTTON & COMPANY
681 FIFTH AVENUE

Printed in the United States of America

To

KATHARINE COMAN

"Quis desiderio sit pudor aut modus
Tam cari capitis?"

ACKNOWLEDGMENTS

Several of these poems, written to my Friend or about her while she was living, are taken from my first published volume of verse, *America the Beautiful,* 1911, now out of print. A few of the memorial poems have appeared in periodicals,—notably in *The Churchman* and *The North American Review.*

PREFATORY NOTE

KATHARINE COMAN, *to whom the following lyrics are addressed, was a teacher and writer of books on political and economic history. A western woman, born in Newark, Ohio, November* 23, 1857, *she graduated from the University of Michigan in* 1880, *and was connected, for the remaining thirty-five years of her life, with Wellesley College. Coming as instructor in English, she went over in* 1881 *to the department of history, serving as instructor till* '85, *and then as professor of history and political economy till* '99. *Dean of the College the following year, she then resumed her teaching, holding the new chair of economics and sociology till failing health necessitated her withdrawal from active service. In* 1913, *having already suffered two critical operations, she became professor emeritus, dying January* 11, 1915.

Classroom routine was, in her case, frequently relieved by years, as well as summers, of travel in Europe and America, with a final trip to Egypt. Her earlier books were very successful school histories of England, but as her interest in economic subjects strengthened, she centered her studies in her own country, spending much time in the South, in Utah, and on the Pacific coast, whence she extended her journeying to Hawaii and Alaska. Her resultant book, INDUSTRIAL HISTORY OF THE UNITED STATES, *proved so valuable a contribution to its subject that the chair established at Wellesley in her honor,* 1921, *is designated the Katharine Coman Professorship of Industrial History. Less than a year before her death, she received urgent proposals from a leading publishing house to prepare a series of volumes dealing with the economic development of our country by local sections,—a congenial task that might well have filled fifteen or twenty years. With undaunted courage she set to work, making pencil notes in the hours least taxed by pain up to within a few weeks of the end.*

But the book which best expresses her vigorous and adventurous personality is her ECONOMIC BEGINNINGS OF THE FAR WEST: HOW WE WON THE LAND BEYOND THE MISSISSIPPI (Macmillan, 2 vols., 851 pp.). *Although her studies had long been pointing toward this book, the author, aided by a Carnegie grant, devoted four years to its direct preparation, following the old westward trails and working, as far as possible, on the ground with original materials. On such scholarly foundation she built a picturesque narrative of vivid human interest, her epic of the pioneers.*

CONTENTS

YELLOW CLOVER

YELLOW CLOVER

MUST I, who walk alone,
Come on it still,
This Puck of plants
The wise would do away with,
The sunshine slants
To play with,
Our wee, gold-dusty flower, the yellow clover,
Which once in parting for a time
That then seemed long,
Ere time for you was over,
We sealed our own?
Do you remember yet,
O Soul beyond the stars,
Beyond the uttermost dim bars
Of space,
Dear Soul who found earth sweet,
Remember by love's grace,

In dreamy hushes of the heavenly song,
How suddenly we halted in our climb,
Lingering, reluctant, up that farthest hill,
Stooped for the blossoms closest to our feet,
And gave them as a token
Each to each,
In lieu of speech,
In lieu of words too grievous to be spoken,
Those little, gypsy, wondering blossoms wet
With a strange dew of tears?

So it began,
This vagabond, unvalued yellow clover,
To be our tenderest language. All the years
It lent a new zest to the summer hours,
As each of us went scheming to surprise
The other with our homely, laureate flowers,
Sonnets and odes,
Fringing our daily roads.
Can amaranth and asphodel
Bring merrier laughter to your eyes?
Oh, if the Blest, in their serene abodes,

Keep any wistful consciousness of earth,
Not grandeurs, but the childish ways of love,
Simplicities of mirth,
Must follow them above
With touches of vague homesickness that pass
Like shadows of swift birds across the grass.
How oft, beneath some foreign arch of sky,
The rover,
You or I,
For life oft sundered look from look,
And voice from voice, the transient dearth
Schooling my soul to brook
This distance that no messages may span,
Would chance
Upon our wilding by a lonely well,
Or drowsy watermill,
Or swaying to the chime of convent bell,
Or where the nightingales of old romance
With tragical contraltos fill
Dim solitudes of infinite desire;
And once I joyed to meet
Our peasant gadabout

A trespasser on trim, seigniorial seat,
Twinkling a saucy eye
As potentates paced by.

Our golden cord! our soft, pursuing flame
From friendship's altar fire!
How proudly we would pluck and tame
The dimpling clusters, mutinously gay!
How swiftly they were sent
Far, far away
On journeys wide
By sea and continent,
Green miles and blue leagues over,
From each of us to each,
That so our hearts might reach
And touch within the yellow clover,
Love's letter to be glad about
Like sunshine when it came!

My sorrow asks no healing; it is love;
Let love then make me brave
To bear the keen hurts of
This careless summertide,

Ay, of our own poor flower,
Changed with our fatal hour,
For all its sunshine vanished when you died.
Only white clover blossoms on your grave.

"SHE IS THE GRACE OF ALL THAT ARE"

"SHE IS THE GRACE OF ALL THAT ARE"

(Ben Jonson)

SHE is the grace of all that are,
  The fragrancy of morn,
The wild, blithe ring, afar, afar,
  Of Dian's horn.

She is the hidden carol in
  The fringes of the wood,
The sudden blue when clouds wax thin,
  The joy of good.

May God who wrought our fleeting race
  Forbid her fatal star,
Remembering she is the grace
  Of all that are.

A MOUNTAIN SOUL

A MOUNTAIN soul, she shines in crystal air
  Above the smokes and clamors of the town.
Her pure, majestic brows serenely wear
    The stars for crown.

The buzzing wings of folly, slander, spite,
  Fall frozen in her alien atmosphere.
Her heart's at home with sunrise and with night
    As neighbors dear

Who tell her ancient tales of time and law,
  The miracle of love breathed into dust,
Until her sweet gray eyes are brimmed with awe
    And steadfast trust.

Remote she dwells mid her celestial kin,
  Rainbow and Moon and Cloud, yet none the less
Full many a weak earth-creature shelters in
    Her friendliness.

She comrades with the child, the bird, the fern,
Poet and sage and rustic chimney-nook,
But Pomp must be a pilgrim ere he earn
Her mountain look,—

Her mountain look, the candor of the snow,
The strength of folded granite, and the calm
Of choiring pines, whose swayed green branches strow
A healing balm.

Oft as the psalmist lifted up his eyes
Unto the hills about Jerusalem,
Did not God's glory with a new surprise
Transfigure them?

That royal harper, passionate for rest,
Held one still summit dearest to his dream,
And only to the golden chords confessed
Its hour supreme;

For lovely is a mountain rosy-lit
With dawn, or steeped in sunshine, azure-hot,

But loveliest when shadows traverse it
And stain it not.

LOVE PLANTED A ROSE

Love planted a rose,
And the world turned sweet.
Where the wheat-field blows
Love planted a rose.
Up the mill-wheel's prose
Ran a music-beat.
Love planted a rose,
And the world turned sweet.

MEASURES

Measure grist by the millful,
Dew by the daffodilful,
April clouds by the skyful,
Tears by Ophelia's eyeful;
Measure leaves by the elmful,
Slaves by the tyrant's realmful,
Green-capped gnomes by the hillful,

Rhymes by Romeo's quillful;
Measure sweets by the jarful,
Dreams by the brooding starful,
Robes by the bridal chestful,
Songs by Bobolink's breastful;
Thorns by the rose's stemful,
Gems by the diademful,
Gold and dust by the cartful,
Only love by the heartful.

WHEN IT BEFORTUNES US

When it befortunes us, who love so dearly,
To hurt each other, let us haste to wring
This joy from our remorseful passioning,—
The wound is witness that we love sincerely.
So slight a weapon, word or silence merely,
Would scarce effect surprisal of a sting,
Were't not thy word, my silence, for we cling
One soul together. Life allots austerely
Unto the rose of love the thorny power
To tear the heart, but ah, love's anodyne!

The prick but proves the presence of the flower,
Our one white rose from gardens all divine.
Then, only then, could grief outlast her hour
Were I ungrieved by least rebuff of thine.

THE VICTORY

THE blue sky at its deepest was pricked by one keen star
That flashed a signal to the moon's uplifted scimitar,
And like a quarrel in a dream we spake with angry breath,
Till in that place of shadows our Love was done to death.

God hung the dawn with carmine and pillared it with gold
To welcome in our new Love, the angel of the old.
With lips still pale from requiems and litanies she came,
But home-sweet lights were in her eyes,—the same, and not the same.

All that was mortal of her, the passion, the caprice,
We had wrapt in cloud-white linen and laid away at peace;
But the living Spirit stood within the temple of the sun,
Her agony accomplished, her consecration won.

MADONNA

ONCE we beheld ecstatic cripples flinging
Away their crutches at a pilgrim shrine.
Do you remember, at the feet divine
Of Mary and her Child, that mother bringing
Her own poor baby-boy deformed, and wringing
Her toilworn hands in supplication? Sign
Of healing there was none; only the whine
Of that repulsive child; only the clinging
Of those gaunt hands. The haloed image stood
Tranquil, unheeding, with its mantle blue
Gathered about that little Christ of wood,
Linen and laces. Then I looked to you

And saw the pure Madonna yearning through
Your pitying face holy with motherhood.

OUR DRIFTWOOD FIRE

How we delighted in our driftwood fire,
When festal eves would merrily decree it,
Dances of rainbow witches high and higher!
We, when this old earth burns, would love to see it.

THE CHANGING ROAD

BENEATH the softly falling snow
The wood whose shy anemones
We plucked such little while ago
Becomes a wood of Christmas trees.

Our paths of rustling silken grass
Will soon be ermine bands of white
Spotted with tiny steps that pass
On silent errands in the night.

The river will be locked in hush
  But frosted like a fairy lawn
With knots of crystal flowers that flush
  By moonlight, blanching in the dawn.

Flown are our minstrels, golden-wing
  And rosy-breast and ruby-throat,
But all the pines are murmuring
  A sweet, orchestral under-note.

So trustfully our hands we lay
  Within the old, kind hands of Time,
Who holds on his mysterious way
  From rime to bloom, from bloom to rime,

And lets us run beside his knee
  O'er rough and smooth, and touch his load,
And play we bear the burden, we,
  And revel in the changing road,

Till ivory dawn and purple noon
  And dove-grey eve have one by one
Traced on the skies their ancient rune,
  And all our little strength is done.

Then Time shall lift a starry torch
  In signal to his gentle Twin,
Who, stooping from a shining porch,
  Gathers the drowsy children in.

I wonder if, through that strange sleep
  Unstirred by clock or silver chime,
Our dreams will not the cadence keep
  Of those unresting feet of Time,

And follow on his beauteous path
  From snow to flowers, from flowers to snow,
And marvel what high charge he hath,
  Whither the fearless footsteps go.

THE DAY IS WANING

THE day is waning; gracious shadows grow;
Sweetness of vesper bells is on the air;
The soul is stirred, a dreaming embryo,
        With impulses to fare
        She knows not where.

Why should we long to live till life become
Dotage or lethargy or feeble fret
Of energies at ebb? When years benumb,
Pierced with the sleep-thorn, let
The dust forget.

But like a song from crumbling folio,
A blossom springing from the broken seed,
Shall not the pilgrim spirit onward go
Whither the bidding lead,
Unfrightened, freed,

Fain of the fresh adventure, trusting Death
As porter in her Father's house, one who
Shall shut the door upon the failing breath,
But lead her safely through
To welcomes new?

For here we pause but in the portico
Of that great temple, radiant with mirth
And beauty, Life. Even as we came, we go.
The ritual of earth
Began with birth;

Doth it not end with birth? From star to star
Shall we not walk the fire who walked the clod,
Nor find the bright, ascending journey far,
Treading, as here we trod,
Handfast with God?

The day is waning; prophesyings blow
Upon the wind; our wondering hearts are wooed
By secret whisperings, and long to know,
Atoms of valiant mood,
Infinitude.

FELICES

We count them happy who have richly known
The sweets of life, the sunshine on the hills,
The mosses in the valley, love that fills
The heart with tears as fragrant as thine own,
O tender moonlight lily, over-blown,
When the inevitable season wills,
By gentle winds beside thy native rills—
We count them happy, yet not these alone.

There is a Crown of Thorns, Way of the
Cross,
Consuming Fire that burns the spirit pure.
By luster of the gold set free from dross,
By light of heaven seen best through earth's
obscure,
By the exceeding gain that waits on loss—
Behold, we count them happy who endure.

LYING TOO FAINT TO LOOK

Lying too faint to look, too spent to stir,
By open window, what a carol came,
The rapture of some scarlet tanager,
As if a voice were uttered out of flame!

THE TRYST[1]

I had come to the trysting place
To meet with Grief.
Like flint I had set my face,
Lest when the dark hour strike
My heart should crumble like
A withered leaf.

[1] Written after the first operation.

Under the aspen tree
  I waited till
The stars made sport of me,
Finding it curious
A soul should shudder thus
  Before God's will.

A bell began to throb,
  And ere it missed
The echo of my sob,
Like silver sunrise flame
Joy through the shadows came
  To keep the tryst.

AT HOLMENKOLLEN

Under our balcony twinkles
The capital city of Norway,
Christiania, toy-like
There in the shimmering spaces
Of her encompassing mountains,
Peeping one over the radiant
Shoulder or crest of another,

Called from their silver recesses
But to glisten and vanish
Back to the borders of Dreamland;
Christiania, only
An incident there in our vista
Of deepening, melting horizons,
Of soft green levels divided
By ranks of spruces and hemlocks,
And pines like tapering spires,
The austere grace of the Norland;
Of isle-flecked waters that chanted
Under the keels of the Vikings,
Where now like butterflies cluster
Tiny white sails and wee playboats
Feathered with smoke; ocean liners
Some of them are, but all dwindled
To elfin similitude under
The mighty enchantment that chastens
Christiania into an item
Of the beauty our balcony watches.

Yet we shall longer remember
The vast ethereal pageants,

Cloud-play and storm-sweep and rain-rush,
All the immense panorama
Of this ever-changeable sky-dome
The crystalline roof-tree of Odin,
Who gleams through his mist-woven curtains,
Who tosses his spear in the sunrise.
We shall remember the coast-fog,
Blurring, enfolding the landscape,
Suddenly shot through with sunshine,
Thinning and dazzling and lifting,
Rising on undulant pinions
Like a white sea-gull upsoaring
To be lost in cærulean distance;
And the moon that glowed like a ruby,
Like a hoarded great ruby the troll-folk
Roll to the feet of Allfather;
And sunsets like tapestry pictures
Of the first strange priest at Christ's altar,
Braving Thor's hammer, amazing
The sea-blue eyes of the pagans
That stare on his vestments embroidered
In gold and in seed-pearl with angels,

Roses of Sharon and crosses;
But longest of all, O Belovèd,
We shall remember the rainbow.

Bifröst the Rainbow, no gossamer
Scarf of a light-footed Iris,
Nay, but the bridge to Valhalla,
Fashioned by gods for the fearless,
Wrought of the blues of the zenith,
Greens of the sea-depth, and crimsons
Forged in the flame-core, forever
Guarded by white-armored Heimdall,
We of the Outlands have seen it,
Bifröst the Rainbow, and marvelled.
For fair it flashed out from the rain-veil,
Bright as if woven of banners,
Broad, like a highway for heroes,
Widening, melting, pervading,
Spreading through space, as our friendship
Colors all life into joyance,
Flooding the sky and the water
And earth with a quivering glory.

Let us be glad of the portent,
For the autumn winds are about us,
The blowing garments of Odin,
And the horn of Heimdall the warder,
Waiting white in the dusk-fall,
Shall blend with the winds in due season
Its unappealable summons.
Oh, then may we do no dishonor
To the hope we have trusted together,
The unbidden one speeding the chosen,
As the uncaressable spirit,
Joy-fellow, grief-fellow, belovèd,
Fares forth alone for the final,
Valorous-hearted adventure,
Over Bifröst the Rainbow,
To the infinite welcome of Godhome.

GOOD FRIDAY IN PARIS

There at the pale feet of the Crucified,
  With not a sob breaking your quiet breath,
You knelt and offered up your body's pride
  And beauty to a creeping, torturing death.

HOW OFT WITH THEE

How oft with thee, Dear Heart Adventurous,
How oft I've fared this foaming deep with thee,
Rejoicing in the splendors of a sea
Never more jewel-shot, more luminous
Than on this strange, swift journey, sweeping us
To our home strand whence, peradventure, we
Shall sail no more, for on that solemn quay
A secret word from God awaiteth us.
Through all the sob that loads our lightest breath,
All wavelike passion of incessant prayer
Beating that shore before we learn thereof
What yet we have to hope or yet to bear,
We stay our breaking hearts on this: Life, Death,
The word is God's, whose every word is Love.

OUR CHRISTMAS TRUCE

WE let you suffer long before we called
  On morphine, life's last mercy, lest
It fail you ere the end; it softly shawled
  Your senses in a luxury of rest,
For Pain, relenting in his long abuse,
  Proclaimed a Christmas truce.

In that brief respite you were light of heart,
  Smiling beneath the wizard wand
That seemed to duel with Death's very dart.
  You felt this Christmas beautiful beyond
All Christmases your shining years had spent,
  So deep was your content.

Even in the presence of your enemies,
  Grim enemies, Disease and Death,
Your cup flowed over. From the forest trees
  Came sprays of pine to shed their spicy breath
On walls and screens where holly boughs made merry
  With vines of partridge berry.

All day the flowers came flocking in until
Their colors glorified your room;
Azaleas flushed each snowy window-sill;
Japonica, carnation blent their bloom;
Violets and roses by you; nearer yet
Pansies and mignonette.

The blue browallia made a patch of sky;
Jonquils and daffodils together
Wrought such a glow of sunshine that the eye
Was dazzled. From afar came purple heather,
Poinsettias, acacia. South and West
Vied which should love you best.

And still they came and still, surprised, you learned
How many wistful loyalties,
How many faiths, affections, friendships yearned
To you and your last Christmastide in these
Farewells from hands you would not clasp again,
These lilies, cyclamen.

You planned our festival from dawn to eve;
  You claimed a morsel of our feast
And gave it to the birds. Each must receive
  The gift that you had hidden in the least
Of evergreens, that crispy, tinselled spruce
  Cut for our Christmas truce.

Wearied by very happiness, you slept
  In your own Paradise of flowers,
Till I, who by your side hushed vigil kept,
  Could almost hope you were no longer ours,
But gone to the unfading gardens, gone
  Beyond the dread of dawn.

HOLY SPIRIT GONE FREE

HOLY SPIRIT GONE FREE

Holy spirit gone free,
  Free of the weary clay,
What do the glad eyes see
  This first day?
Where is Heaven for thee?

Art thou adoring the Throne,
  Kissing the Wounded Feet?
Art thou greeting thine own,
  Souls home-sweet?
Whither, O whither flown?

Art thou lingering here,
  Still, as aforetime, fain
Sorrow of mine to cheer?
  In this pain
Art thou the courage, Dear?

STARRY RUNAWAY

No, no, Belovèd; starry runaway,
  Even my heartbreak would not call thee back
To this pain-wasted majesty of clay,
  But help me bear it,—bear this almanac

On thine own desk, that tells me yesterday
  Thy voice was still my courage, thy gray eyes
My joy, and sets in desolate array
  The months to come. Yet thy far enterprise

My own belated soul shall soon essay,
  In the pity of some certain hour set free
To seek my Life. 'Tis but a threshold stay,
  A task or two, and then I'll follow thee.

THE GOD OF SILENCE

THE God of Silence, at whose ancient shrine
  The Persians worshipped, was it thou, O
    Death,
Thou who wilt grant thy favor, stern, benign,
  For no less offering than pulse and breath?

CREMATION

Let the fires be swift, not slow.
In the terror of the glow
Let the awful change be wrought
Till the flesh is light as thought.

Will the spirit not pause and wait
For her wonted faring-mate
If it follow as pale motes may
Up the slanting sunbeam way;

If it drift as ashes might
On the fragrances of night,
By that one white breath of heat
Shriven to pure and sweet?

IF THE CELESTIAL BODY

If the Celestial Body, ethereal, mystic, remembers
Your Brunhild splendor of youth,
If this that sprang up like a flame from the perishing mortal embers
Is you in truth,

Angel face that looks with your eyes and lifts
your brows under
The oldtime glistening crown
Of hair like the sunrise gold, face touched with
child-wonder,
Look down, look down,

If not through forbidden rift in the sky,
through some ivory casement
Of dream in the sobbing night,
And draw, as of old, my spirit from sorrow's
selfish abasement
To love's delight;

For the swiftest gleam of your radiant glance
in the unreturning
Years of our mortal grace
Would flood my heart with fulness of joy. Oh,
lean to my yearning,
Celestial face.

IF YOU COULD COME

My love, my love, if you could come once more
  From your high place,
I would not question you for heavenly lore,
But, silent, take the comfort of your face.

I would not ask you if those golden spheres
  In love rejoice,
If only our stained star hath sin and tears,
But fill my famished hearing with your voice.

One touch of you were worth a thousand creeds.
  My wound is numb
Through toil-pressed day, but all night long it bleeds
In aching dreams, and still you cannot come.

WHY WANDER MORE?

Why wander more? My dreams have folded
wing;
Old longings for far beauty melt in grief.
The pathos of all life, all withering,
Is in the dancing of an April leaf.

YOUR OWN PLANTS BLOOM AGAIN

Your own plants bloom again,
Azalea, cyclamen,
Japonica, all keep their rendezvous
With Christmas in the sun.
Ah, but you,
Whose Christmases are done,
The heart of all the room,
Where does my darling bloom?

IN CEDAR HILL CEMETERY
(Newark, Ohio.)

WEARILY up the unfamiliar way,
A traveller that cannot cease to crave
The happiness your welcome ever gave,
I come, Belovèd, at the ebb of day,
To keep my promised tryst with your far grave.

The sunset lingers on the serried stones
Of your home-gathering kindred, those who quaffed
Life's fullest cup, and babies epitaphed
For love, not deeds. Fluting his twilight tones
A robin perches on the tapering shaft.

O ashes, memory of mortal love,
Sealed in your urn beneath the greensward, pure
From all disease and all decay, secure
From evil, what am I to weep above
Your beautiful and tranquil sepulture?

The shadowy cedars climb the hill, all rife
With whispers, that are less the wings of birds
And stir of sprays than murmurous, dim words.
Ah, death may comprehend them, but not life,
Dark embryo that still the shell engirds.

The two tall, sentinel white birches sift
The soft blue skylight through serrated leaves,
Lest shadow should too soon, too deeply drift
Between your silence and my heart that heaves
With its vain longing, while the quails uplift

Their ringing calls from the dusk fields below,
Heralds of joy on very edge of night.
The eternal tide of stars begins to flow,
Flecking the gloom with points of golden light,
And I, whose task is long, arise and go.

Is it you that follow me and fold me fast
With your old comfort, quieting the strife
Of stormy pulses, as in sorrows past?
There is no sorrow but is peace at last.
God grant there be no death that is not life!

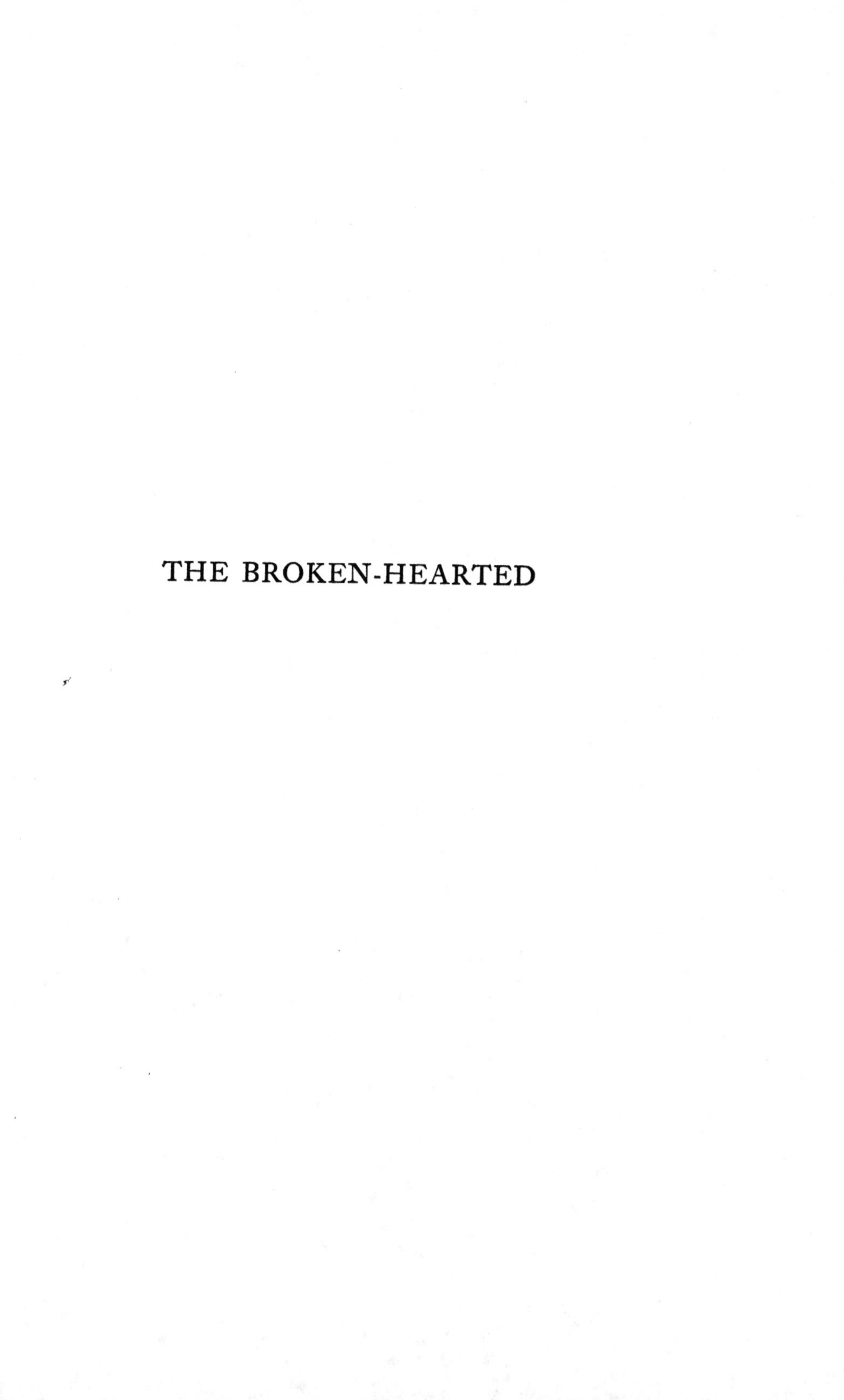

THE BROKEN-HEARTED

THE BROKEN-HEARTED

O STRANGE, hushed fellowship of those
Who tread a darkened star,
Who breathe the fragrance of the rose
And thrill with pain instead
Of that old joy, long dead!

Amid earth's hurrying throngs they move
Like spirits from afar,
Exiled from their one land of love,
Lost as a flood-whelmed leaf,
Initiates of grief.

They give the mystic countersign
In glancing looks that are
Illuminate with lore divine,
Each anguish whispering each
Closer than household speech.

Each casts his hard-earned alms into
The other's craving jar,
A grain of wisdom garnered through
Wild, weeping storms, pale peace
That blooms where longings cease.

No badge they wear to worldly view
—These of the hidden scar—
But on their foreheads is the dew
Anointed eyes may see
Of dark Gethsemane.

FIREWOOD

First was a fire of myrtle,
  Just for my Love and me;
The storm at the door might hurtle,
  But safe within sat we.

Now cypress boughs are burning
  Upon my hearth, and all
Whose hearts are sore with yearning
  May share my forest-hall.

LIFE

LIFE went hand in hand with Joy
  Ere Life's heart was broken,
This round world his magic toy
  Fashioned to betoken
Some bright mystery that glows
Jubilant in star and rose,
Allah's fair incognitos.
Life kept holiday with Joy
  Till Life's heart was broken.

Now the star and rose but seem
  Forecasts of their fading,
Pathos of a slipping dream,
  Ruin masquerading
In a fragile gold and pink.
Life bends brooding o'er the brink
Whither stars and roses sink,
Life to whom all beauties seem
  Forecasts of their fading.

SHUT OUT

DEATH bars me from my garden, but by the
dusty road
Glints many a vagrant blossom the wind's
caprices sowed.

Death locks my door against me and flings the
golden key
To sink with many another beneath the moan-
ing sea.

But there are haunts for gypsies upon the
heather moors,
Where we share with one another the lore of
out-of-doors;

And gypsy tells to gypsy what healing herbs
are best
When the old wound starts a-throbbing and
starlight brings no rest.

THE PATH OF SORROW

The path of sorrow is no lonely path;
Through every rock defile hushed footsteps grope;
No thorny covert that its winding hath
But prayer is there and fellowship of hope.

WORK

O Work, drab angel, lead me day by day,
A tired slave contented to obey,
From task to task, by hand so firm and cool
It quiets fever. Thus from life's long school
At last I'll earn my quittance and away.

A ROSE-WHITE CLOUD

A rose-white cloud that blossoms in the blue,
Opening its curly petals one by one,
Joy of divinest beauty, thrilling through
A weary heart where even pain seemed done.

FAILURE ON FAILURE

Failure on failure seed the slow success.
All mired and bruised the footsore traveller
came
By swamp and steep, through unimagined
stress,
To envied fame.

Sorrow on sorrow purge the selfish heart.
Not till our dearest are caught up above
Our hurt, our help, we learn life's finest art,
The art of love.

A FROSTED BUSH IN THE SUN

An arsenal of diamond spears,
A rainbow splintering
Into a million points of sheen,
A little blazing Troy.
Its beauty stirs the pool of tears
As by an angel's wing,
Troubling the waters with a keen
Revivifying joy.

POINTED FIRS

DULL clang that hurts this dreamy air,
  Forgive me if I turn
From you to little bells of dew
  Upon the forest fern.

More lightly may I lift my prayer
  Beneath these pointed firs
Imbued with simple sanctitude
  By woodland worshippers.

The squirrel saints race up the stair,
  Frisking from bough to stem,
For God finds no behavior odd
  In wild Jerusalem.

I love the liberty they wear,
  Those green, soft-chanting spires
That hush to hear the hermit thrush
  Voice earth's divine desires.

Broken by grief, I cannot bear
  The ministry of words,
Content to taste the sacrament
  Of winds and leaves and birds.

BIRDS AND BOOKS

ALL day these ruby-throated humming-birds,
Illiberal elves,
Draw honey from the bee-balm at my door
And offer me no share.

All day the poets with melodious words
Delight themselves,
And of their graciousness my strength re-
 store
For sorrow I must bear.

LAUGHTER

THE daily commonplace our mirth would
 brighten
With twinkling as of saffron butterflies
On yellow-blossomed bush of indigo,
But to the solemn joy beyond the skies,
That crystal sphere no sun nor stars enlighten,
Can Laughter come? The sages answer no.

Then, Laughter, in my lonely heart still tarry,
A sweet and bitter fool, and gently break
Your quips and whimsies on this brooding
Grief
Till he arouse. Ay, even for Sorrow's sake
Stay with us that our burden we may carry
More lightly for your loving disbelief.

YESTERDAY'S GRIEF

THE rain that fell a yesterday is ruby on the
roses,
Silver on the poplar-leaf and gold on willow-
stem;
The grief that chanced a yesterday is silence
that encloses
Holy loves where time and change shall never
trouble them.

The rain that fell a yesterday makes all the
hillside glisten,
Coral on the laurel and beryl on the grass;
The grief that chanced a yesterday has taught
the soul to listen
For whispers of eternity in all the winds that
pass.

O faint-of-heart, storm-beaten, this rain will
gleam to-morrow
Flame within the columbine and jewels on the
thorn,
Heaven in the forget-me-not; though sorrow
now be sorrow,
Yet sorrow shall be beauty in the magic of the
morn.

WESTERING HEART

WESTERING HEART

Westering Heart, Restless Heart, Heart of the Pioneer,
Still I wonder, wonder, what is Heaven to thee;
Lover of far horizons, eager to bring them near,
Journeying Heart, Yearning Heart, rover of land and sea.

What can stay the feet we knew,
Springing feet our meadows mourn,
From adventuring the blue
Undiscovered bourne,
Where the stars, God's wild canaries,
Sing above the ether prairies,
And the dream of time flows on
To illimitable dawn?

Tender Heart, Defender Heart, bowed with the
wide world's woe,
Bearing thine own grief lightly, lightly as
mortal might,
Shedding on dim, steep pathways the courage
of thy glow,
Gleaming Heart, Redeeming Heart, a torch
against the night;
Not the peace of Paradise
Long can hold thee, ransomed, blest,
From the old, glad sacrifice,
From the unforgotten quest,
On the wastes remotest, barren,
Watering the Rose of Sharon
Till the bleak and bitter sand
Blossoms into Holy Land.

Lifted Heart, Pain-sifted Heart, that madest
death a psalm,
Pallid with sore suffering, yet kissing still the
rod,

Hushed and held within some great encompassment of calm,
Soaring Heart, Adoring Heart, to whom "it all is God,"
What though precious gem on gem
Build the shining Zion walls,
Christ is thy Jerusalem,
Wheresoe'er His service calls.
O our Star, at rest in motion,
Lost in light, as wave in ocean,
May thy ministering bliss
Still remember what we miss.

TO ONE WHO WAITS

I COUNT the years by Junes that flush our laurel,
Our clustered bushes at the corner-wall,
And coax the crinkled buds to spread their small,
White chalices pricked out with rose and coral.
Slow are the seasons, yet I may not quarrel
With beauty. Dawns and stars, blossoms that foam
Enchanted orchards, where the orioles call,
Green leaves that flutter, golden leaves that fall,
Cloud caravans of snow will bring me home.
I count the years by Junes that flush our laurel.

What changes chronicle the life eternal?
Beyond the starry archipelagoes,
How do you calendar the stream that flows,
Forever singing, from the Throne supernal?
For as in wheat the sweetness of the kernel
Is ripened with the sunshine more and more,

Let sorrow trust, where mortal wisdom knows
Nothing, ah nothing, that the love of those
Who made earth heaven is greater than before
And watches for us in the life eternal.

If human love be but the soul's rehearsal
For that high harmony so piercing sweet
Its rhythm is pulsing in the wildest beat
Of passion, in the quietest dispersal
Of household blessings, Love the universal
Music of being, must not, Dear and True,
Our love that longs in me still yearn in you,
New-christened at the wide-winged Mercy seat
To a redeeming grace, my Paraclete,
For the divine accord my soul's rehearsal?

I count the years by Junes that flush our laurel,
And you, perchance, in some shy interspace
Of Paradise, have found a woodsy place,
A bit of wild that welcomes fern and sorrel,
Where mystery of moss and prickly moral
Of briar-rose may spring in finer bloom,
And Time's old witchery so far presume

That you, impatient for the glad embrace,
May now and then a dewy footpath trace
To see if June again has flushed the laurel.

THE GATES OF DEATH

Marmoreal, impregnable,
  Immutable, we bear
The searching shafts of human thought,
  The onset of despair.
The indistinguishable cell
  Of spirit and of brain
Through all the centuries has fought
  Its puny fight in vain.

The pageant of humanity
  Dissolves as on it falls
The shadow of our bulwarks dense,
  Our unrevealing walls.
Its starcraft is but vanity.
  Its aspen faith but blows
In winds whose whither and whose whence
  No mind of mortal knows.

Yet is there one strong battle-lord
  Who still the day retrieves.
Ashes and dust are infidel;
  His very life believes.
Forever is his only word.
  Breath is incredulous,
But Love, undaunted, terrible,
  Demands his own of us.

LOOKING ON THE MILKY WAY

Flood of stars that hold your course
High across the night,
Serried lustres numberless
As the souls that Godward press
In continual flight,
From what flaming wildfire source,
Shimmering river of the skies,
Tide of light,
Do your waves arise?

Toward what fatal fall does your
Flowing current gleam,
While those flocking souls ascend

Ever upward? For what end
Can there be to love?
Only in faith that loves endure,
We, a momentary race,
Dare to dream
Spirit outsoars space.

IMMORTALITY

THE Angel of the Sun
    Had spread a wing of flame
        Athwart the orient sky;
Then grew my spirit one
    With Beauty and became
        A Joy that could not die.

At some far torch of gold
    The shining soul was lit
        And claims celestial kin.
Shadows its house enfold,
    But are not one with it.
        The splendor bides within.

Sorrow and vain desire
Are drifts of darkness gone
Upon the ebb of night.
Spark of the primal fire,
Bliss wakens with the dawn,
Light answering to light.

THE LUXURY OF EASE

The luxury of ease comes after ache;
Joy of reunion cannot be except
By pang of parting; only death may break
My way to you whom I so long have wept.

I WILL NOT FEAR

I will not fear the Valley, for amid
The blur of the innumerable dead,
Your glimmering footsteps cannot be so hid
But I shall follow in them, homeward led.

WHEN AT THE LAST

WHEN at the last I lift my lids to brook
The close-bent face of Death, perchance I'll see
Your wide, sweet eyes, with their eternal look
Of childhood, smiling through the mist on me.

WHERE TIME'S LONG RIVER

WHERE Time's long river hushes in the sea,
Beyond the furthest coast of starry space,
I dream that my far traveller waits for me,
Poised like a bird in glad, impatient grace.

WHITE ROSE

WHITE rose, white rose,
Thou that art
All my garden,
Walled, apart,
Grief my white rose,
Thorn in heart!

WHITE ROSE

White rose, pale
As brooding star
Over Arden,
Where dreams are!
All shall fail
That is not far.

White rose, white rose,
No storms beat
On thy petals,
Blooming sweet,
Love my white rose,
At God's feet.

White rose, what
Is mortal fate,
Rain and nettles?
Roses wait.
Death is but
The garden gate.

NOW MY LOVE IS FLOWN AWAY

Now my Love is flown away
  Earth wears another semblance,
Opal dawn and turquoise day,
  Stars and moon and sun
Conscious are and mystical,
  Jewels of remembrance,
Keepsakes from the festival,
  Our festival that's done.

Now my Love is flown away
  The air is full of calling,
Dewy voices that allay
  Thirst and dust-annoy,
Tones that haunt the hall of Time,
  Crystal echoes falling
From some far, ethereal chime
  Whose bell-ringer is Joy.

TESTIMONY

I, WHO am deaf and blind,
  I, lame and weak,
  Listen and seek,
Follow and find;

Yet have no word to say
  What I have found,
  Clearer than sound,
Brighter than day;

Wings in the heavy clod,
  Beauty in pain.
  Even the chain
Bindeth to God.

WHAT IS THE SPIRIT?

i

WHAT is the spirit? Nay,
We know not—star in clay.

We know not, yet we trust
The dream within the dust.

We trust not, yet we hark
The song within the dark.

ii

These few bewildered days
Ask little blame or praise.

All mortal deeds go by
As cloudlets down the sky.

We are our longing. Thus
Let Love remember us.

iii

We know not whither beat
Its wings, nor what defeat

Death's mighty muffling glooms
May cast on fluttering plumes,

Or if it be success—
That folded quietness.

iv

When like a flaming scroll
Earth shrivels, if the soul

Should those fierce heats outwear,
What of ourselves were there?

A longing bruised and dim,
A seed of seraphim.

IN BOHEMIA:

A CORONA OF SONNETS

IN BOHEMIA

A CORONA OF SONNETS

(I)

I GIVE you joy, my Dearest. Death is done,
Your martyrdom accomplished, and your crown
Of sainthood, woven of such pains as drown
Remembering eyes in tears, superbly won.
No stain upon your faith's white splendor,
none;
No moment when you cast your courage down,
A broken sword. You enter with renown
Out of these shadows into radiant sun.
Gone, gone; yet still we pore upon your face,
Your face already strange in sculptured pallor,
Listening, but not to us; your face, a scroll
Frailer than parchment, where we yet may trace
A holy script. O loyalty! O valor!
Your voice still echoes: "Bless the Lord, my
soul."

Your voice still echoes: "Bless the Lord, my
soul,
And all that is within me, bless His name!"
All, all within you? The disease, the shame
Let loose in your pure body sweet and whole
Beyond the wont of flesh, till evil stole
On those unconscious tissues, torment came
As furtively as some slow-creeping flame
Corroding from within the golden bowl?
Yea, verily, your body's bitter woe
In your divine endurance blessed the Lord.
Your youth of bounding pulses, one clear choir
Of joy and strength and glorious desire,
Could lift no strain of adoration so
Poignant, angelic, suffering's master-chord.

Poignant, angelic, suffering's master-chord,
Your music rings through my bewildered days,
A worship, and my spirit strives to raise
Thanksgiving with your own, above this horde
Of griefs, rebellions, yearnings. Oh, afford
From your rich joy, in your old, generous ways,

Largess to me, that my torn heart may praise
Death, even Death, your healing, your reward.
Death entered, bearer of the only key
That could unlock the iron gates of pain.
The Angel of the Lord, our very love
Knelt in his shining, as he smote the chain
From off your limbs, and swift you rose, set free,
Forever free. My heart, be glad thereof!

It was heart's woe, Most Beautiful my Friend,
To watch your bright hair wither, shoulders bend
Beneath the burden. White as carrier-dove
Your numb, forgetful hand, an empty glove,
Lies on a quiet breast the hard gasps rend
No longer. From the broken cage ascend,
God's homing bird, to boundless air above.
Your joy shall be my joy,—ay, though the word
Chokes to a sob. My tragedy is done.
I could laugh upon the stroke even of Orion's

Great, gleaming sword, dull by comparison
With that keen pang unbearable that heard
Your only moan: "My soul is among lions."

Your only moan: "My soul is among lions."
You were on shipboard, sailing home to die.
I sat beside you on the deck; the sky
Glistened with constellations, starry scions
Of an eternal fire. Not white-hot irons
Could so have seared my spirit as that cry
From your deep anguish. You will know me by
That scar through joys of all imagined Zions.
You, you, so light to leap, so fleet to race,
Eager for burdens, I must see you shorn
Of all those ardors, slowly dispossessed
Of your proud heritage, turning your face
Toward Death, your face each dawn more wan, more worn.
I could not make him an unwelcome guest.

I could not make him an unwelcome guest,
For that dim morning, when I raised the shade

Upon the joy of sunrise, you essayed
To look with eyes that pleaded but for rest,
So weary, O so weary. Peace was best.
Yet as Death hushed the breath, your love delayed
His touch an instant, while your white lips made
Effort to smile on me, a last behest
Of courage. Ah, such little time before
In panting torture you had lifted arms
To me for help I could not, could not give;
Yet in your utmost weakness, you restore
My fainting strength. Delivered from all harms
In your deliverance, Dear Heart, I live.

In your deliverance, Dear Heart, I live.
The olive cross you loved for Bethlehem,
Slipt under your chill hand, with lily-stem,
Merges in your mortality. We give
Your tired beauty, wistful, fugitive,
To chariot of fire. Your requiem

Is chanted. Prayer and holy apothegm
Are uttered. All is ashes, where no sieve
Shall find forever form or face of you.
But in your upper chamber, in your own
Bohemia, wide-windowed to the sun,
We are together, all our suffering through,
Our long suspense and dread a shadow flown.
I give you joy, my Dearest. Death is done.

(II)

Our word shall still be Joy, shall still be Joy.
Death shall not be a frost that blackens all
The blossoms in our garden. Love, I call
To mind your life on earth, so to employ
My aching thoughts, lest lurking grief decoy
My spirit from its vow. And yet they fall,
Slow tears, on even this cramped, childish scrawl
Of hidden verses that you bade destroy.
Where is that child, with wide gray eyes of wonder

And broad braids yellow as the prairie moon
Whereon she gazed, suggesting with sage thrift
To cut it into stars would be a boon,
'Twould make so many? Ah, sweet childhoods, plunder
Of Time's fast wings, an April petal-drift!

From Time's fast wings, an April petal-drift
These songs have fluttered back, secretly penned,
A murmurous joy, deep in the leafy bend
Of silver-maple or in fragrant rift
Of haystack. Were these ten small leaves a gift
From Father's desk, this desk become my friend
As it was his and yours? Did Mother mend
With magic thread these rough-torn pages whiffed
Down half a century that changed the child
From form to form, a maid for men's desire,
Scholar with quarreling books about her piled,

Far traveller, sufferer, ashes on the pyre?
How fierce an anguish to the spirit brings
This mocking immortality of things!

The mocking immortality of things
Shall be forgiven to this tiny tome
For its dear childishness,—epic of home,
Ohio farm with joy of watersprings
And cedars full of crystal carollings;
Slow cows to drive and cosset lambs to comb;
Sheep deftly yoked to turn the garden loam
For labor-saving brothers; venturings
Of emulous fleets that sailed the orchard brook,
The proudest topped by mousetrap cabin where
A frog sat skipper with a pompous look.
Such hours are of their beauty unaware,
White daisies dancing in a meadow nook,
Till wistful memory beholds them fair.

Your wistful memory beheld them fair
And still more fair as further they receded,
Those childhood scenes dawn-colored and dew-
beaded.

All needments but few luxuries were there
In that true home,—joyance of sun-steeped air,
Tasks bubbling into frolic, hearts that heeded
High voices, eager summer days that speeded
To tranquil twilights. Grouped about the chair
Where Mother with her mending took such rest
As mothers may, on doorsteps fronting west
Father and lads and lassies watched the strange
Drama of sunset, glimpsing crown and wing
And many a cloudy shape swift vanishing
By nature's mandate of eternal change.

By nature's mandate of eternal change
That group has melted, like those shifting gleams
Of air, a vision, one of many dreams
That haunt the levels of that lonely grange.
The soldier father was the first to range
Beyond the sunset, he whom war's extremes
Had wellnigh shattered, who from battle themes

Turned sharply, as from thoughts he would
estrange.
The children's games of war he could not
brook.
Their Shiloh with small fallen heroes woke
So deep a horror in his brooding look
They ceased to play at slaughter, yet no less
Joyed to behold him honored of the folk
For manhood, as his wife for graciousness.

Hers, when I knew her, was the graciousness
Of one long regnant on the quiet throne
Of love,—such love as tender children own
For parents whom the heavy years oppress;
Such love as she in turn poured back to bless
Their varying ways with steadfast music,
known
From cradle-time as life's sweet undertone,
The mother-love, unfailing, measureless.
And forth from love there blossomed such
high graces,
Courage and courtesy, joy, wisdom clear,

A fortitude forbidding all complaints,
That while she walketh now in heavenly places,
I think the very stars must hold her dear
And do her reverence as a queen of saints.

You did her reverence as a queen of saints
Many glad years together. When she passed
Beyond your touch, your faith still held her fast,
And as our human longing ever paints
Its Paradise with flush of earth, and faints
Before sheer spirit, so in that dread vast
You saw her waiting, loving arms outcast,
In the old happy doorway. What constraints
Were those that led your brother's questing feet
To even such homestead on a Berkshire hill
For your last summer? Winds across the wheat,
Frolic of calves, familiar farm employ
Closed up your circle, while our word was still

—O breaking hearts!—while still our word
was Joy.

(III)

I could not bear my grief but that I must.
Is it not you who live, while I am dead,
Cold as that stone whereon the fire was
red,
Now left alone to lichen or to dust?
"Thoughts of a Stone" your title has it, just
A bit of baby lyric, yet you said
What here I prove,—the campfire glows are
spread
And trampled, picnic over, not a crust
Of joy dropt for the stone whence flames rose
bright,
So bright it deemed itself a thing of fire.
And I must bear this grief night after night,
Day after day, through weeks and months and
years,
This grief become myself, too dull for tears,
Bewildered past all pain, past all desire.

Bewildered past all pain, past all desire,
I stare forever on a snowy scene,
Blue glint of crusted drifts, the irised green
Of frost-filmed pines, impertinence of spire
And joy-lit panes, till shoot of anguish, dire
As crematory heats within whose keen
Embraces dies your beauty that has been,
Stings me to consciousness. Then I inquire
Of my forgotten senses, and I learn,
Noting accustomed walls and voices near,
I am no longer tranced in that return
From white Mount Auburn, where we left you,
Dear,
—No, no, not you; a worn-out robe to burn,
Even as this globe shall gleam and disappear.

Even as this globe shall gleam and disappear,
My life has vanished, life of joy I led
Folded in yours. Never again to tread
The station platform, tired scrutineer
Of every face, until a sudden cheer
Tingles through all my veins, fatigue is sped,

For you are with me, sweet as daily bread,
Refreshing as cool water! Oh, the mere
Touch of your hand, your hand that now is
ashes,
Turned all the day's vexations into mirth.
Beside you in the car, its groaning pull
And grinding brakes and harsh metallic crashes
Made blither music than remains on earth;
And yet I wonder I am sorrowful.

I wonder I am sorrowful, for now
There is no pain to fear for you. The sting
Of death is drawn. Escaped from suffering,
The crown of thorns is lifted from your
brow.
I wonder I am sorrowful, for how
Can I be warped with winter, when the spring
Floods your free spirit, and its raptures wing
Your golden flight from our bare mortal
bough?
Yet, Ever Dearest, I am sorrowful,
If apathy be sorrow. I receive

No joy of beauty from this snowflake wool
That wraps so tenderly each writhen tree,
Now that your tenderness is gone from me.
Stark selfishness of sorrow! Yet I grieve.

Stark selfishness of sorrow! Yet I grieve,
Vaguely aware of watchful loves that hold
Their warmth between me and the utter cold.
Patient and generous and wise, they leave
Me here alone with you and grief, yet weave
Sweet walls of roses round us, paly gold,
Soft pink, clear carmine, white, in manifold
Pattern of petals; mossy buds men thieve
From Elfland, high-blown hearts of joy, tall
stems
Crowned with great flushes. In our own rose-
garden
We are together and I take reproof
From your dear voice that would not have me
harden
My soul against such blessing. Love condemns
The sorrow that from love would walk aloof.

The sorrow that from love would walk aloof
Implores forgiveness even while it sins.
One heart is home; the many hearts are inns
With glow of festal joy, with sheltering roof.
Your life was of my life the warp and woof
Whereon most precious friendships, disciplines,
Passions embroidered rich designs. Grief
wins
Pardon from love for very love's behoof.
For true love knows that love must still be true,
Not kind pretender nor blind self-deceiver.
It matters not what other mourners do;
I turn that nectar cup I drained with you
Down on the board. No more shall there be
Weaver
Of Rainbows in my heaven's too tranquil blue.

No Rainbow Weaver in my heaven's calm blue;
The magic gate through which each common
thing
Came shining with a strange transfiguring

Is sealed. Where now shall Grief keep rendezvous
With Comfort? Nay, I would not learn the new
Who crave the old,—our water from the spring,
Not sacramental wine. The seasons bring
But phantoms of those joys that died with you.
Years pass. The household feasts your old-time guests.
A rose casts shadow on the cloth. Ah, thrust
Of hidden hurt amid the flying jests!
For that dark, silent image to my seeing
Is memory-ghost of your warm, fragrant being.
I could not bear my grief but that I must.

(IV)

Do you remember still your dear-loved earth,
Shadows of stormy clouds that sweep across
Old, castled Heidelberg; the golden gloss
Of sands atoning to the Sphinx for dearth
Of ancient splendors; strange Hawaiian mirth
At arbor feast, where, heedless of their loss,

Their vanishing, those blithe brown folk would
toss
Wreathed heads to music, as if life were worth,
Even on such sliding brink, its hour of joy?
Do you remember how the sunsets burned
In Norway skies? Not pain itself could cloy
Your wild-bird heart that ever longed to roam,
That ever for the bluer distance yearned
And on each bough of beauty was at home.

God's bird, upon his every bough at home,
With skylarks on a Devon cliff between
The purple moors and purple sea, in green
Swiss valleys, in fair Florence, royal Rome,
Amid grim totem-poles by frozen foam;
Poplars of France that follow her serene,
Broad rivers; Andalusian groves, with sheen
Of orange and pomegranate, 'neath the dome
Of drowsy convent or above the game
Of choral children; bells of Brittany
Pouring their joyous gloria upon
The villagers, whose piety must don

To please the Saint their quaintest finery.
Horizons flushed about you when you came.

Horizons flushed about you when you came.
Our low skies lifted and the world looked in.
Joy-fellow of the journeying sun and kin
To that wind-god whose feet were plumed with
flame,
Still, scholar, teacher, still your steadfast aim
Was understanding of the ways that win
Men upward from a blind, brute origin
To ordered peoples. Ever would you claim
That in our own crude country glows romance
Whereby the elder charm of Europe fades.
Falls of the Rhine you deemed Undine's dance
To great Columbia's thundering cascades,
Prophets that from her cloudy palisades
Summoned the pioneers to glorious chance.

The pioneers who took that glorious chance
You traced o'er plain and mountain, hunters,
trappers,

Gold-seekers, prairie schooners with child-nappers
In mother's arms, babes whose inheritance
Of virgin land in limitless expanse
Was won by hero fathers,—daring tappers
Of earth's hid treasuries, unconscious mappers
Of new dominions for mankind's advance.
Their courage beat like joy within your pulse.
Sleeping delicious hours of night away
On a Pacific beach mid shells and dulse,
Children beside you and a young moon beaming
Upon the surf that splashed you in its play,
Even then of their adventure you were dreaming.

Always of their adventure you were dreaming,
Retreading their hard paths and poring long
Over their crabbed scripts, with patience strong
As zest itself, until your mind was teeming
With frontier lore. I laughed to hear it streaming,

Untiring as the red-eyed vireo's song,
From lips folk called reserved nor did them
wrong;
But silence had at last its full redeeming.
Your earlier volumes had but blazed the way
For this, your own heart's book, your joy of
toil,
To be of all your glad achievement crown.
I watched the gold fruit ripening day by day
And felt your dream's incredulous recoil
When merciless disease would face it down.

Not merciless disease might face it down.
Through those four years beset with wasting
pain,
The surgeon's knife again and yet again,
Our spring of joy slow withering to brown
Autumn of ruin, still your dream, like town
Stormed by resistless armies, would not deign
To lower its proud banner. So we twain
Finished your book beneath Death's very
frown.

For all the hospital punctilio,
Through the drear night within your mind would grow
Those sentences my morning pen would spring
To meet, while guilty mirth flashed to and fro
From your brave eyes to mine, for joy and woe
As comrades climbed your height of suffering.

Joy climbed with woe your height of suffering.
Oft in your clouded eyes, as if soft-kissed,
Pleasure would brighten, banishing the mist
Of weariness, while from past journeying
Kind memory would many a picture bring,
Your Rockies robed in sunny amethyst,
Or that stupendous canon, annalist
Of all the æons. To your heart would cling
Sweet, showery Aprils with their miracle
Of leaf and blossom, frozen nature's birth
Into fresh loveliness. Again the spell
Of Italy was on you and you smiled

As when you caught her songs from singing
child.
Do you remember still your dear-loved earth?

(V)

Do saints go gypsying in Paradise?
How merrily, escaped from golden street
And jasper wall, your footsteps light and fleet
Would rove the wildwood—wood whose happy
spice
And balm conceal no treacherous device
Of trap to snare and shatter small furred feet,
Where no shot bird beats broken wing! Oh,
sweet
To taste a joy not bought by sacrifice!
Have you, as on Lake Ripley, bungalow
By water's edge, where from your sunrise bath
To twilight hymn the saucy chipmunks strow
Your floor with shells, scolding in frolic wrath
To see you sweep them forth? And up your
path
What other heavenly callers come and go?

What other heavenly callers come and go
To hear your voice, my best of music hushed,
To rest beside the lake on ledges plushed
With moss and watch the tall marsh rushes
blow,
Red-shouldered blackbirds flashing to and fro
Above the water-lilies, and the flushed
Breast of the robin guarding nest soft-brushed
By dancing linden leaves? Do cherubs know
Your welcome, as so many children here
Have known it? For you ever used to say
Their joy of laughter was your perfect cure
For weariness. You were so tired, Dear,
Before you died, please God that now with pure
Spirits of childhood you keep holiday.

Spirits of childhood, keeping holiday
On your broad steps that to the rippling lake
Descend, would call on Sigurd to awake
In his low grave. How could our collie stay
With earth, when you had fled so far away?
Our most adoring lover! For love's sake

The seal of death's enchanted door would
break,
And Heaven be gladder for his winsome play.
With what a joyful plunge he would chase the
stick
Flung forth into that little sea of glass!
How proudly swim with it to shore and flick
A crystal rain on scampering cherubim;
Then, well content, your hand caressing him,
Stretch on the threshold, greeting all who pass.

Over your threshold eagerly would pass
Your blessed dead, on furlough from employ
In that new life where service still is joy,
Parents and sister and the baby lass
Your arms once cherished, now in wisdom's
class
So high 'tis hers to train with starry toy
And many a bright, angelical decoy
Your own celestial infancy. The grass
That never withers feels the drawing nigh
Of two dear brothers, yet unused to wend

The ways of Zion, but of instinct true
To find the violet path that leads to you,
And with the later fares a laughing friend
Whom Sigurd springs to meet with lyric cry.

Only for her he lifts his lyric cry,
Lady of Cedar Hill, yet proffers paw
Full cordially to all who, by the law
That brings our own to us at last, though sky
Must melt between, your threshold glorify,
—Our Pearl of Wellesley poets, who would draw
New dreams from Plato; Lincoln, not a flaw
Left on that beauty angels know him by;
Francis the Pitiful, and our vesper bell,
Christina, who while still on earth knew well,
Even as the psalmist king of Israel,
Heaven's joy of harping,—words of hers rose faint
From your pale lips, the last ere silence fell,—
And One with Whom your soul was best acquaint.

That One with Whom your soul was best
acquaint,
The wandering Christ Who loved the cedar
trees
Of Lebanon, the red anemones
Of Carmel, Whose low bidding put restraint
On stormy waves, Who fled from the complaint
Of hungering multitudes to shores like these,
Reeds shaken with the wind, may He not please
To come to you, His follower, His saint?
O Joy of Joys! Beatitude complete!
I see you kneel to anoint those wayworn feet
With ointment from your alabaster box
Of precious faith. But straightway doubt
strikes chilly
Across the heart and my poor babbling mocks.
How may the earth-blind bulb behold the lily?

How may the earth-blind bulb behold the bliss
Of lilies, dance and color, odor, air?
Or iridescent wings their joy declare
To that dark prisoner in the chrysalis?

Thought reels before the metamorphosis
Of mortal to immortal. Lest despair
Rob us of strength for burdens yet to bear,
We tease God's inconceivable with this
Mere childishness of query upon query.
Have they no need of us who need them so?
Do they never, of eternity grown weary,
Long for the river-song of Time's onflow?
Can one tree, even the Tree of Life, suffice?
Do saints go gypsying in Paradise?

(VI)

No more than memory, love's afterglow?
Our quarter century of joy, can it
Be all? The lilting hours like birds would flit
By us, who loitered in the portico
Of love's high palace. Time enough to know
Its court decorum, nor would mind admit
Love's term of learning was not infinite.
Ah, courtesies my carelessness let go!

Then you forsook me ere my love was wise,
Not wise enough to know if still you are,
Too pure a light for my enshadowed eyes,
Or if, unconscious of my very grief,
Your vanished spirit, beautiful as brief,
Be quenched in darkness, like a shooting star.

Quenched in deep darkness, like a shooting star,
Or hidden as the moon within a cloud?
How often have we watched her, silver-browed,
Engulfed by gloom, and soon, upon its far,
Joy-brightened rim, emerge without a scar
On her pale splendor? Do you wear your shroud
So lightly? We but know that disallowed
To mortal vision is your avatar.
Nay, I must journey past all moons, all aid
Of these discarded senses, past all space
And pealing rhythm of time, ere I be made
Spirit to apprehend your spirit face;
Yet of this only is my soul afraid,

That you are merged in some transcendent
grace.

If you are merged in some transcendent grace,
Drowned in divinity, ah, then no more
We are ourselves, no longer shall implore
The Power that rushes on its own proud race
Toward terrible perfection at a pace
So passionate that we who would adore
A Father are but bubbles on the roar
Of that tumultuous tide. If such strange case
Be ours, if unappealable decree
Make human love and joy and suffering
A whirl of autumn leaves, heart's mockery,
Speak it, O Science, with authentic voice,
And let us end it now. For who would cling
To such existence, serve such God, by choice?

I choose to serve my hope of God, a hope
Like to the shipwrecked mariner's, whose frail
Boat lurches while he leaps to calk and bail,
Make fast his water-keg with shred of rope,

Still searching, searching, dizzy eyes a-grope,
The blank of ocean for a saving sail.
Not his the fault if whelming seas prevail;
What courage can, he does. So would I
cope
With our immensity of doubt, with all
This vast incertitude on which we toss,
Hoping, and striving in the hope I cherish,
Till nought remains to solace or appal.
If hope be truth, 'tis joy. If all be loss,
What matters it to life brought forth to perish?

To life brought forth to perish what is
life?
Nought recks the field-mouse peeping from a
loop
Of grasses that this evening may bring swoop
Upon him of the owl whose plaintive fife
We echo for our sport. No dread of knife
Troubles those sheep that sedulously droop
Their heads above the clover; even this group
Of calves frisk forth to market without strife.

Wild, pirate hawks cry loud above the caw
Of scandaled citizens, yet hawks and crows
Alike obey commandments that we call
Instinct. In joy the flood of being flows,
Each life the food of higher life, and all
Creatures of earth, sea, air accept the Law.

Why may not we in joy accept the Law?
Is thought a curse that we still chafe in vain,
One blind link more in an unending chain,
Against such doom? We see that children draw
Life from their parents; empires, wisps of straw
On a swift stream, swirl by that man may gain
A firmer basis for a nobler reign;
And yet we would extinction overawe
With our dim spark of God. Oh, what are we,
That in the face of all we witness, still
Clamor and cry for immortality;
Dare to withhold our puny homage till

Some oracle shall tell us if there be
A Will within the Law, and Love that Will?

O Will within the Law, O Love the Will,
To Thee I lift what faltering faith I may,
Longing allegiance fain its vow to pay
In Thy vast temple, but of little skill
To parley with Jehovah. Still, O still
Let her be my interpreter and pray
The prayer I cannot; let as yesterday
Her faith's clear fountain feed my wavering rill.
O yesterday, and all its joy of you!
Just back from morning run, bright locks a-blow
About flushed face, such gladness gleaming through
Candid gray eyes as deepens them to blue,
Arms full of blossoming branches fresh with dew,
You come to memory, love's afterglow.

(VII)

Your sentence by my quavering voice was told.
Amazed, like the forsaken Christ, you viewed
The spectral shape of your appointed rood,
Even as when once autumnal mists unrolled
And gave you, unsuspecting, to behold
For the first time the Alps. Stricken you stood,
Awed, terrified at their bleak magnitude,
And shivered in the sunshine, smitten cold.
But straight you turned, so gallantly that God
Was proud of you, from ways you longed to wend,
From all your joy of life to this new goal,
Resolved to die with honor. Firm of soul,
Wresting a victory from defeat, you trod
Your Via Dolorosa to the end.

Your Via Dolorosa was mine own.
I walked beside you, far as love might go.
I saw, while mortal beauty dimmed, the glow

Of spirit brighten, till the soul had flown,
As birds at some cærulean bidding, known
Only to wings, fly south before the snow
To joy of summer. Left behind, below,
I wait till clouds of time be overblown.
Yet is there not a Way, a Truth, a Life
That my dull, darkened heart may reach you
    by?
Are not these walls, that watched your passing,
    rife
With mysteries that on me call and gleam?
Is it no more than pain's importunate dream,
Or do I sometimes feel your presence nigh?

Have I not sometimes felt your presence nigh?
You said: "I will not leave you comfortless,"
And oft half conscious of a swift impress
Upon my spirit, lights that clarify
A problem, calm on storm, ever I try
To hold my listening heart in readiness
For joy of your impalpable caress,
Wisdom of your inaudible reply.

Oh, still shed blessing on me from those wings
Of whose soft tarriance I would be aware,
Light intimations, fleet evanishings,
Speech finer than all syllables, a rare
Shining within my soul, a thrill intense
That breaketh not Death's law of reticence.

It breaketh not Death's law of reticence,
For when I would my miracles declare
They melt as sunset colors in the air
Of evening, and myself oft wonder whence
Came to my heart that brief intelligence
Of a communion eyes and ears forswear
And touch denies. My ebbing joys despair
And charge imagination with pretense.
Is this my lonely camp by love patrolled,
Or am I fooled by credulous desire?
What hand throws balsam on my bivouac fire
When it burns low? Whose is the tender tone
That hushes grief with courage, as of old:
"We will be strong and glad in love alone"?

"We will be strong and glad in love alone."
I can endure through all my desolate days,
But can I share your canticles of praise,
Your adoration at the Great White Throne
That rises for the pure in heart? Can moan
Mount up to singing? How shall summer raise
Beauty from these your ashes? Shall the maize
Ripen in gold where willow-herb was sown?
By seven springs has your far grave been grassed,
And in my depth of sorrow are astir
New powers, perceptions, joys, against my earth
Uppressing, secret agonies of birth,
At bidding of their angel gardener:
"The Life Eternal! Let us hold it fast!"

"Let us hold fast the Life Eternal!" So
You bade me, so I strive, a better lover
Than I shall be a saint. Oh, starspace rover,

Would we might stroll once more, as long ago,
Startling the bobolinks, across the glow
Of Wellesley meadows lit by yellow clover
With "God in all," you murmured, and "God over
All beauty and all joy"! For as I know
Your soul enfolding mine, you dwelt in Him,
Dwelt in the Light of God. How clearly fall
On memory your words, when once your breath
Waited the ether, and my eyes went dim!
"Oh, have no fear, Dear Heart, for life and death
Are one," you smiled, "and God is All in All."

Forevermore is God your All in All.
In His eternal radiance you dwell,
Fulfilling His High Word as sunbeams quell
These earthly shadows. In your dying, gall
You tasted, felt the spear your flesh appal,
Were crucified with Christ, but it is well

With you at last in that bright citadel
Pain cannot storm, beyond the shining wall
Grief may not scale. That terror of all men,
The gate of gloom, is now your gate of gold.
Sore-tested, your heroic heart has won
The pearl of peace. More quietly than when
Your sentence by my quavering voice was told,
I give you joy, my Dearest. Death is done.

www.ingramcontent.com/pod-product-compliance
Lightning Source LLC
LaVergne TN
LVHW021420110826
845150LV00007B/2017

* 9 7 8 1 4 2 5 5 0 9 0 4 0 *